LET'S TALK MARRIAGE

LET'S TALK MARRIAGE

A Guide for Couples Preparing to Marry

F. Dean Lueking

William B. Eerdmans Publishing Company
Grand Rapids, Michigan / Cambridge, U.K.

Wm. B. Eerdmans Publishing Co.
255 Jefferson Ave. S.E., Grand Rapids, Michigan 49503 /
P.O. Box 163, Cambridge CB3 9PU U.K.

Printed in the United States of America

06 05 04 03 02 01   7 6 5 4 3 2 1

Library of Congress Cataloging-in-Publication Data

Lueking, F. Dean (Frederick Dean), 1928-
    Let's talk marriage: a guide for couples preparing to marry /
F. Dean Lueking.
        p.   cm.
    ISBN 0-8028-4904-0 (pbk.: alk. paper)
        1. Marriage.   2. Marriage counseling.
    3. Marriage — Religious aspects — Christianity.   I. Title.

    HQ734.L784   2001
✓ 306.81 — dc21
    L   200103322

www.eerdmans.com

Contents

Foreword, by Martin E. Marty   1

Introduction   9

UNITY OF MINDS   17
Understanding Each Other's
Ways of Thinking

     Money   18

     Family   22

     Friends   27

     Communication   35

     Shared Interests   41

THE UNITY OF YOUR BODIES   45

*Giving Yourselves to Each Other
as Male and Female*

Formative Experiences Early in Life   49

The Teen Years   52

The Case for Fidelity and Commitment   53

Levels of Intimacy   57

Becoming Parents   64

SOULS UNITED IN MARRIAGE   69

Building a Spiritual Foundation   69

Marriage as a Mutual Ministry   73

Communicating Upward — Together   78

Finding Your Church Home   81

Till Death Parts You   84

Foreword

Let's Talk Marriage will both prompt and help advance conversation on the second-most important topic that is likely to come up in the lives of the American majority. First, of course, is one's relation to God. Second, for that majority which marries, is one's relation to the spouse, a relation that, if it goes well, helps further positive interaction with all the other people who need and deserve love of a sort different than that we know in marriage.

Let's Talk Marriage is a friendly book. Couples in love and those who love couples in love will do well to make noise about it so that it can be of help to many. If you are half of such a couple, picture drawing up a chair in the quiet of a pastor's study, as a couple thousand couples have been privileged to do where Dr. Lueking hung his pastoral shingle. Then picture becoming engaged in talk about your engagement. Guarantee: you will find it rewarding and, if followed, quite possibly decisive in helping you get marriage off to a promising start. Which means you will have resources to help you anticipate the non-promising, even threatening days that shadow most marriages.

Let's Talk Marriage is precisely that: a talk, a bidding to invite couples to talk. Talk implies conversation, which is different from argument. Argument occurs when two people know they have the right answer to a question or have taken the right position. Each then sets out to defeat or humiliate or expel or convince or convert the other — your choice among those "or's," and there are many more. Argument has its place in high school debates, high court decisions, and high-risk legislative choices. Rarely does it help couples prepare for marriage. Conversation is between two people or, here, among three — Pastor Lueking will emerge from these pages as not only a talker but a figurative and intense listener — who approach an issue and let it be dominated not by cocksure answers but by concerned questions. How will we best prepare for our marriage? How will we contribute to its fulfillment and success? The book implies give-and-take.

Let's Talk Marriage is a serious book. The adjective "serious" might throw some possible readers and users off from the beginning. There are good reasons why seriousness first offends but then, as in the present case, attracts. Here is partly why: pre-marital counseling, which is what this book is about, differs from marital counseling in that people choose to engage in it when they ordinarily do not have a problem, or have not yet recognized it.

When I am sent to a counselor, perhaps by a marital partner in time of troubles, I know I am in serious trouble, and I want serious counseling. A smile is welcome, but taking things lightly and making them joking matters ruins the climate and the prospects. When I choose to go to a pre-marital counselor, along with a probable marital partner in times of high romance, I enter a climate in which people like to banter, to titter nervously, to provoke titillation, and to duck the serious stuff.

I write this in a time when many couples seek celebrity or notoriety or try to make their momentary splash by inserting trivial at best and comic at worst elements into the pre-marital and marital mix. We see televised pictures of marriages with couples on roller coasters and water skis and on cliff sides. We read of pranks played not to enhance the enjoyment of all but to use cruelty as a way of distracting from the serious things that fun marriages will be.

Any of us who have done pre-marital counseling, even if we have engaged in it hundreds fewer times than Dr. Lueking, have our stories to tell. My mental bank includes the only counsel I received — we had no one bidding my fiancée and me with something like *Let's Talk Marriage* — from a medical doctor. One had to go in for blood samples and all those things the state required. In the world of 1952, when counseling in general was a less frequent and less advanced art, I was wise enough to the world to know that counseling, for example about the sexual side of marriage, did go on. I must have been wise enough to know that I had things to learn.

The examination took five minutes. The doctor leaned back against a high white table and told me everything was fine. There was an awkward pause. I broke the silence with the shortest response to the *Let's Talk Marriage* kind of invitation by mumbling a question: Was there anything he had to offer by way of advice about the sexual side of our imminent marriage?

"Yes," he said. "Don't be rabbits."

That was all.

This occurred in the era of large families, and the empathetic doctor foresaw that we would be entering a scene in which birth control was less openly discussed or quietly pursued than it would be a few short years later. Don't multiply the way rabbits do. (We ended up having four children, which was not being like rabbits in the norms of that day and not not being like rabbits by the measures of the present time.) A month later I became an assistant to the sage pastor who preceded Pastor Lueking in a River

Forest, Illinois, pulpit. In many informal ways he offered the kind of serious counsel that my wife and I
craved but were denied by a wisecrack from a doctor.

One more: I had become pastor-at-a-distance to
a couple preparing for marriage. They had asked me
to come out of retirement, as it were, and "do the
honors" as friend and cleric. The groom was in his
sixties, the bride in her forties, the marry-er in his
fifties. From that vantage, I assumed that in my ver-
sion of *Let's Talk Marriage* we did not have to talk
about their having children.

Flown to the foreseen scene of the nuptials and
with a couple of hours set aside for friendly counsel,
I thought I would break the ice with a light approach. I said something like, "while neither you
nor I are Roman Catholic, let me start formidably
by paraphrasing Catholic rules, which include: every conjugal act has to have a procreative intent." In
other words, you can't get together unless there's a
potential that your expression of love can issue in
conception. One of them responded: "Well, what
are we waiting for?" I believe it was nine months
and a few days after their wedding that a child
came along. But it was not nine minutes after our
bantering exchange that things turned serious and
we talked about matters of body and soul, the ma-
terial and spiritual, heart and spirit, tragedy and
comedy — and all the other things that *Let's Talk
Marriage* opens one to.

Let's Talk Marriage has a Christian presumption. That does not mean that non-Christians cannot get a great deal from the book. It does mean that couples in which one is Christian and the other is not, really should reckon with it. I almost envied Dean Lueking for his ability to assume this Christian foundation. As a professor at a university best described as secular-pluralistic — aren't they all? — and an ordained minister, I would on numerous occasions be called in to counsel and "perform" when couples came up with combinations such as Christian/Baha'i, Christian/Muslim, Christian/a-theist. Paradoxically, however, I found these problematic ones occasions for truly serious exploration of faith and faiths.

Let's Talk Marriage is addressed to couples in a culture where over 80 percent of polled people identify their "preference" as Catholic or Protestant or Evangelical or Christian in general. But a large percentage of that number do not move beyond preference to commitment. Preference can often mean nothing more than knowing how to find the church your daughter has not been in since her baptism, but toward whose physical setting you and she have strong attractions. *Let's Talk Marriage* is not a document promoting proselytization or evangelization. But I think and hope it will help couples of any age take seriously the fact that becoming a part of a faith community, or deepening one's commitment to such a community, is not only intrinsically valuable but a great boon to marital happiness.

One year after the late Cardinal Joseph Bernardin came to Chicago he was asked to address a large gathering of Protestant clergy. One could see that he was reading from his own handwriting on a yellow legal pad. He had taken the event seriously. He surprised the audience by saying that he showed more interest in the documentation the archdiocesan office received from couples, one of which was Catholic, than any other official documents. Some of the reports and questionnaires suggested that the bride-to-be (or groom, just as well) had a rough idea of which one her parish ought to be because she wanted to be married there. Partner's religion? "I'm not sure. He's not a Catholic. I think he'd probably be some sort of Protestant, maybe Methodist or Unitarian or something like that." The Cardinal worried about the future of faith and marriage in such instances.

Far preferable were those cases in which the couple signaled: one of us is Catholic, much involved with faith and parish; the other is not, but is much involved with his or her faith and congregation. How will we work this out? The pair would not be arguing but they were conversing. The Cardinal did not drop an expected other shoe and tell how the priest counselor should make a Catholic out of the "other." He left that open to time, imagination, the integrity of the couple, and the Holy Spirit.

Let's Talk Marriage leaves many issues similarly open. Its author trusts people who are concerned enough to read it and to follow up on its clues — and then seek a personal pastoral counselor to advance the conversation. Such counseling will not be of the sort to which one had to be sent. It will be a matter of free choice, and serious, and, yes, in the end, friendly and fun. I picture the Holy Spirit hovering over such conversations, such couples. Let's talk. . . .

Martin E. Marty
Emeritus, The University of Chicago

Introduction

To marry.

To borrow an overworked adjective, what an *awesome* decision you've both made!

I am glad to be among those who congratulate you and wish you well as you prepare for something so monumental as the rest of your lives together as husband and wife. I especially want to invite you to prepare well for your future together.

This marriage preparation book is written to help you deepen and broaden your communication as you prepare for marriage. To be sure, you both have already thought and spoken a great deal about your present and future. The following pages are meant to give you specific ways to increase the art and skills of confirming those things about which you are already confident and of recognizing things that need attention. As I envision you as a couple continuing to talk together, I would like to join you via these pages as a friend and guide. Here is a way that can happen.

First, please set definite times apart for sharing this book, in manageable time segments that suit you both, and find someplace where you will not be disturbed. Then, and I urge you strongly here, read the book aloud to each other, alternating paragraphs or short sections as you choose. Take as long as you need to proceed this way. Reading aloud to each other may seem awkward at first. But there is a reason for doing so. It is to let you hear each other speaking, not just thinking or wondering or guessing, but speaking things of foremost importance for the years ahead, both large and small. Doing this now is valuable practice in developing the trust and maturity that will enable you to open up to each other at those deeper levels of mutual enrichment. Can you think of anything more important to you now, anything worthier of the priority of time and effort this requires?

As you get into the book you will notice questions at regular intervals. At those points, please lay the book aside. Instead of looking at a page, look at each other and find your way into the particulars of what each of you thinks and feels about that subject. It's not necessary to nail down everything about everything, of course. It is necessary to get a clearer, truer picture of how each of you envisions your respective roles, assumptions, expectations, and hopes, as well as problems and uncertainties. In this way you hear more than words. You are sharing your openness and your vulnerability and discovering that it's safe — in fact wonderfully freeing to do so. You are letting each other in on your real strengths and the weaknesses you need no longer hide. You build mutual confidence for your marriage because misgivings are pried loose from deep inside where they could one day erupt with full-blown, blind-siding force because they were buried in denial. You entrust to each other your fondest dreams and help each other find ways to experience them as realities rather than pipe dreams.

By all means, then, don't hurry or shortchange yourselves in this most important thing you can do now and later in marriage: communicate! That's the whole point of this book, which will have value for you in direct proportion to the extent to which you explore the as yet unexplored, as well as strengthen what is already secure. The latter builds confidence for the former.

Look forward to this preparation journey before you. Besides being important, such conversing is really enjoyable. Let it be fun and deeply satisfying These coming hours of talking together are second to none in long-range value — and they don't cost you a cent! As the wedding approaches the days will get busier. The pressure to put this kind of preparation off will tighten. But look at it this way: nothing, absolutely nothing, is more promising now than experiencing your mutual love in the form of open, honest, caring, purposeful communicating in mind and heart. It's the surest path to a marriage that is solid, lasting, and happier in ways you cannot yet envision.

It may be that you live in geographically distant places and cannot frequently be together to read through the book. Don't let that hamper your preparation. Get a copy for each of you. Jot down notes on the page margin as you read. Compare them by phone or e-mail. When you're together and the time is short, put a priority on those notes you've made that will set the conversation agenda. Be creative in finding every possible means to focus and enrich your shared thoughts. After all, it's your future and you want to be at your best for each other — for the rest of your lives.

I must speak a frank warning to you as two people preparing to marry in a society in which failed marriage has reached epidemic proportions. One out of every two marriages ends in divorce. In nearly every case that statistic is traceable back to little or no serious preparation for the high calling and hard work of marriage. The tragedy is that people sail into marriage as though simply going through the motions ensures happiness, settling for poor communication that gets poorer as the realities of married life come along. Finally it dies in divorce. It's not just poor communication that kills marriage, but the absence of anything substantive to communicate. That sets people up for stagnation instead of the character growth that sustains married people through thick and thin. Thus family, friends, and the wider network of human relationships are deprived of marriage as the main building block for all human community. If you are a divorced person you know the pain of that loss and never want it again. If you are a widow or widower, you know the weight of the words "till death parts us." Along with a blunt warning about the horrific pressures that work against you, please accept this appeal to give each other your best in preparation. See clearly what is solid and lasting as well as what must change and drop away as you start well toward a marriage in which you will never cease marveling that you have each other — and never regret that you ever married in the first place.

It's a very good idea to meet with a trusted pastor, priest, rabbi, or competent third person as you prepare. That person may well have marriage preparation materials to offer in addition to this book. Gain all you can from every source.

This book is written from the perspective of the Christian faith, but with no intent to limit its benefit only to those who share this outlook. Do not feel disadvantaged if you are an outsider to serious

Christian belief or a long-time absentee from faithful worship and practice. Be open and mutually considerate of each other's spiritual roots, and ready to do something about the lack of them. Is there any good reason to miss the unique opportunity this momentous time in your life offers for renewed spiritual life as fertile soil in which your love for each other can grow?

Use these pages as a road map, then, starting with realism about where you are now and your willingness to work well together toward where you want to be. In a one-sentence summary, the basic theme of the book is that good marriage consists of lifelong growth in unity in mind, body, and soul. It's pictured in the diagram on the facing page, which includes the particular topics connected with each aspect of unity.

One thing more. I write from over four decades in pastoral ministry and from the experience of preparing well over a thousand couples for marriage. I acknowledge my debt to many of them, from whom I have learned much in observing how good preparation led to marriages of beauty and depth. I also write as a husband happily married to my wife, Beverly, for over four decades. I gratefully acknowledge my indebtedness to her for so much of what may speak to you in these pages — something due in no small part to her love, her qualities, and her commitment with me in the covenant of our mar-

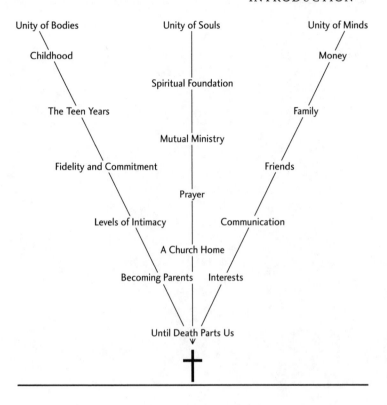

riage. The book is a thank you and salute to her. We both hope to keep on learning and growing with you in this God-given vocation that at its best is an earthly taste of the eternal wedding feast with Christ in the life yet to come. That, to borrow again the overworked adjective, is indeed *awesome*.

F. Dean Lueking
Oak Park, Illinois

Unity of Minds

Understanding Each Other's
Ways of Thinking

It is no small miracle that each of you, with your distinctive ways of thinking, can come to a unity of your minds in this vital area of marriage. While love is the motive for probing deeper here, it never requires that two people think exactly alike. No two people can. What love builds is the willingness and skill to really want to understand the other, to accept, negotiate, fight fair, work through, and come out with mutually satisfactory agreements that show you've heard each other with care, goodwill, and awareness of how you help each other grow.

Before you are important areas to help confirm and expand your thinking together on practical matters in marriage. As you read to each other, pause for taking up the questions that tailor the subject to your interests and needs.

Money

Are you a good money manager? Don't be shy about it if you are. The checkbook or savings account status tells the facts. If you are, you are. And that's good. Don't be coy if you're not. Many a single person is used to letting the bank statement square up the monthly mess of too-casual bookkeeping (I speak from experience). Indifferent money management is a red flag waving. Recognize it now.

Which of you will keep the books and pay the bills? How will you set up your financial handling, a joint account or separately? In either case, why? Have you given each other a full and complete picture of your finances? Income(s)? Savings accounts? Debts outstanding? *Take the time you need, now, to go over these items.*

One of the first ways you've experienced how your mind works is in handling money. Where to go when eating out and what to order. What to do for entertainment and what to wear and what to drive are items you're getting familiar with. It's normal to want to impress each other with what one is happy to spend on the other. I remember flying my fiancée to the city where I lived, though it about did in my checking balance for the month. A certain amount of that goes with the territory of courtship and there is something wonderful about the cockeyed spontaneity and fun of it.

Wowing each other with spending is hardly the essence of thoughtful money handling, however. Think of the responsibility of paying for the wedding, which can either be a lifetime highlight or a nightmare of excessive spending. Take care for each other's views as you decide on announcements, wedding dresses, tuxedos, flowers, rings, church fees, the reception (location, menu, guest list, music), limo, photographer, video, the honeymoon, etcetera. For sure, you want the great day to be fine in every way. But think it through carefully and as you do, be alert to each other's strengths and weaknesses in money matters. Weddings are among the major expenditures of marriage and it comes at you right off the bat. Count on it, there will be stressful moments as you plan it all out.

By all means, set a wedding budget. Be clear about who pays for what. Be equally clear about assumptions of family help in footing the wedding bill. Parents who can and do help financially may also assume entitlement to take charge of planning. This is unwise and needs straightforward, diplomatic clarity about the fact that you both need to keep the upper hand in wedding plans. Budget accordingly. Take on your responsibilities gracefully. Be each other's confidant. Tell each other everything. Take nothing for granted. Get it all down on paper and keep a sharp eye on costs that can grow beyond your means all too quickly.

Time for talking specifics: Do we have a budget? Who will keep the checkbook? Pay bills? Are we together on wedding plans and payment? Are we fully informed about each other's salary, savings account, indebtedness? What needs more time for negotiating, decision-making?

If you have been married before, and especially if you have children to support, the financial side of that needs clarifying. If you have a will (and you both should) or if an estate plan is set up that promises support to those who need it, explain the plan and allow plenty of time for any questions. Well-planned support arrangements for children reflect the blessings of previous times in life and normally should not be changed. Let the people involved know now that your marriage will not mean loss of support for them. Start anew as a new couple, pooling your resources in ways that will not jeopardize existing commitments and needlessly cause hard feelings among those who are just getting to know you.

The idea of a pre-nuptial agreement when there is no previous marriage or family commitment is troubling to me, largely because I have seen it become a document of distrust. Clear, mutually agreed upon, fair financial arrangements in the case of death or disablement are essential, of course. Pre-nuptial agreements, which virtually assume divorce — and who gets what — are something else, and they raise serious questions about whether the marriage should take place. This much is sure: if you cannot be sure your fiancée is not out for your money, or your fiancée assumes that you have such motives for marriage, don't get married. Better to settle that basic question now rather than later.

Money management involves giving as well as getting. That's easy to overlook and therefore important to think about now. Wise and generous giving, of money and lots else, is a sign of character and maturing faith. It is not automatic by any means, but a learned art. Most single people are understandably geared to spending mainly on themselves, though not exclusively by any means. You learn something of each other's thinking about giving when customary times arrive for gift-giving: birthdays, anniversaries, and other special occasions. It broadens out when you think of giving as an act of faith in support of the church and the spread of the gospel, for philanthropic purposes in and beyond the community, for alumni associations of schools that served you well, for special interests and volunteering of your time and talent as well as your money for the wider good. Be thoughtful of each other's background, or lack of it, in matters of giving, for we all bring baggage with us. The great thing is to grow together into faithful, intelligent giving, a source of rightful satisfaction. Never let money become a weapon or a bribe. You must rule it, or it will surely rule you. *All clear — or not yet?*

Family

Marriage links your families as well as continuing them through your children.

You are getting onto that as you get to know each other's families and find your way into new relationships with in-laws. It's normal to feel somewhat tentative, even on trial, in the early stages. Your respective families feel something of the same. Another common experience is to always be at your best in their company. There is nothing wrong with that if it reflects an inherent respect for the family into which you are entering. If it is a continuing façade, however, it's phony and something other than good manners. Being at home with each other's families moves beyond manners to levels of mutual acceptance in the face of the flaws that inevitably surface. "Why do your folks think this . . . or do that?" is not necessarily a hostile question. It can be an honest inquiry and deserves a good answer.

Deep-rooted feelings are involved in growing toward compatibility with each other's parents and siblings. In-law jokes abound, but in the end they are not funny. No matter how hard to take a family is, it is still the family of your loved one. Love does not willfully put them down or stereotype them, but makes room for the long journey toward understanding and acceptance. Love does not assume instant acceptance nor hurry the use of emotion-laden words such as Mom or Dad.

Have you met your future in-laws? How is it going? What's encouraging? What's not? What can each of you do to improve things?

Here is an interesting way to spend some time in getting a deeper look at what you bring from your families. The diagram on page 24 invites each of you to list the positive and negative qualities of your parents, and previous generations if you can. Jot down the first half dozen traits that come to your mind and then tell each other which of them, positive and negative, you recognize in yourself.

Each of you is the next edition of the genetic pathway of inherited traits. As you interpret these things to each other, take the subject a step further. Tell each other the parental traits, if you know the parents of your fiancée, that you recognize in them. Those qualities are likely to grow as the years advance. Make it for better not for worse.

Air the dirty family linen, please. This is not to gossip or blame, but to understand. Alcoholism, depression, marital breakups, genetic diseases, penny-pinchers, spendthrifts, the family embarrassments, and the whole nine yards, lay it all out. And cer-

FATHER	−						
	+						

MOTHER	−						
	+						

FATHER	−						
	+						

MOTHER	−						
	+						

tainly speak the whole story of family successes and accomplishments of which all are rightly proud. Tell of the unsung heroines and heroes who quietly held things together through hard times. Tell each other stories of family lore and traditions that you hope to continue in your household. What memories return of fun times as kids, of love shared, of dreams realized? Who in your family has sacrificed for you and made it possible to reach goals that seemed unreachable? Through such exchanges you give to each other something priceless: the heritage that weaves a family fabric of beauty and strength. *Lots to talk about here; go at it.*

No doubt you are already in on the tricky matter of giving equal time to each family; the challenge grows as time moves on. Whose family do we visit this holiday, birthday, or vacation? Be fair with each other. Learn how to negotiate through patience and love what can be stormy waters if selfishness prevails. Overbearing parents can pose the problem of possessive, overdependent claims upon their children. It's tough because no one wants to confront such problems head-on at this stage. But the main thing is that you are both clear about what the issues are and doing your share in resolving them. Conversely, overdependence on parents can appear when apron strings are not clearly cut, as they must be. Cutting apron strings is not abandoning your family of origin. It is defining the new relationship so that a new reciprocity can grow. It is God's plan that a man and woman leave father and mother and cleave to each other. As you are open, respectful, and loving to each others' families now, you are building a foundation that will support a great deal in the future, including an aged, ill parent who needs your wisdom and love in making decisions of all sorts. Or you may need your parents when calamity hits your marriage hard. God alone know what's ahead. Let it suffice for now that you both are spotting problems now and dealing with them as best you can. Even more, you are noting blessings as new families come together in relationships that already now hold promise for greater blessing in years to come.

When couples who marry bring children from previous marriages, no single formula ensures flawless transitions. Little or no preparation of the children is cruel and asking for trouble. Patient, intelligent, loving acceptance of children at a pace they can handle is what counts, and for that the best in parental communication is crucial. Common sense says the birth parent must be careful against overprotectiveness of the children; the new parent must guard against over-permissiveness in allowing mayhem to develop. As a blended family, take the time and make the effort required for blending. Be with them in activities of their interest. Give them room to adjust. Agree on the ground rules for disciplining young children; stick with the boundaries the teens normally protest against but need — more than they might talk about. Lay out times for children living with the divorced parent. Keep time that you need for yourselves as new parents, and do so without guilt. Love will make the passage to new family unity possible. It will not happen without time and hard work, but it's good work and time well spent. *If this paragraph applies, talk of what's encouraging, discouraging in blending a new family so far. If it does not apply, read on.*

Friends

Both of you bring previous and continuing friendships into your present and future. Think especially of friends who are more than acquaintances. These are a treasure beyond price, and now comes the prospect of sharing that treasure.

Beware the assumption that your closest friends are going to be your spouse's choice as well. That is not a given, of course. Keep in mind that you have long since accepted and been accepted by your close friends, warts and all. But your loved one is just beginning to feel the chemistry of this or that person's place in your lives. How you think about each other's friends may seem marginal at the moment because of geographic distance or the press of these busy days. But how to assimilate friends, old and new, into your marriage is still of importance to you both.

I learned something about this from my parents early in my life. My mother's closest friend was a brilliant but eccentric person whose intellectual acumen and artistic bent endeared her to my mother, but not to many others. My father found her plainly odd and much too talkative. Mother realized that Emma Lou would continue to be her best friend but not in the same way to my father. Dad worked hard at patience, with varying success, concentrating on her good traits and putting up with the rest. I'm sure my parents found ways to negotiate this uneven relationship to a mutual understanding. Mother did not overload the schedule with inordinate time with Emma Lou. Father was not rude or begrudging of the time (mostly by phone as I recall) the friendship took.

Can you think of parallels? Obnoxious traits such as a loud mouth, bigotry, drunkenness, drug abuse, or offensive flirting must not be excused as just the way it is. Putting up with that kind of stupid behavior at the expense of your spouse sends the message that the other person is more important than the person you are to marry. It may be the beginning of second thoughts that cancel the marriage, and rightly so. Be careful about friends who, for some obvious reason, do not fit into the marriage and don't force what doesn't fit. *Does anybody, anything, come to mind here?*

Conversely, what a great gift your true friends are to your marriage! They bless you with qualities that enrich you for a lifetime, qualities you will naturally emulate, and it will be a two-way street. Already now, such friends brighten your leisure time and enliven conversation and shared interests. You know you can count on them in crisis times, even as they can count on you. Sometimes such friends are closer than family, with no judgment implied on either. A saying puts it strikingly: "We are friends and we have friends so that we don't get killed" — figuratively, if not sometimes literally true. Welcome the enormous influence that good friends offer: mutual enjoyments, confidences shared, good habits learned, values established, faith imparted. In the increasingly urban settings of our lives, such friendships are ever more precious because few places can be lonelier than a crowded city with no friends. Loneliness is a major ailment of our times. If one or both of you have jobs that take you away for long hours, good friends can help you stay sane and human. *Does this make sense? How much do friends mean to you? Who are the friends who you both delight to be with? Are there others you need to talk about?*

You not only have friends, you are friends to each other. Sound preparation for solid marriage surely makes a husband and wife deep and lasting friends. Put into practice those things in each of you that make for friendship: love, kindness, generosity, patience, forgiveness, courtesy, loyalty, availability, empathy, thoughtfulness, mutual interests, and being an interesting person.

You will be making new friends as well as keeping continuing friendships. Two key qualities make for rich and lasting friendships: trust and respect.

First is trust. As you choose friends it is inevitable that you will compare yourselves to those who are close to you. Is our place as nice as theirs? Our car as good as theirs? Our income as much as theirs? Our work as impressive as theirs? Our talents up to theirs? etc. No one and no couple is totally exempt from jealousy, or at least from some sense of competitiveness with friends. It is your love that keeps your trust in each other's sufficiency above the blight of jealousy. Keep reassuring each other that the achievements of others are fine, but pose no threat in reducing either of you to whining complainers. Guard like the plague against sentences that begin with "If only we had it as good as . . ." Trust means being happy together for what you are and gratitude for what you have, not unhappiness that you don't have what others have.

Trust extends to a problem area of friendship that has to do with sexual infidelity, which reaches epidemic proportions these days as cinema and television soap opera flaunt it as the norm for healthy behavior between consenting adults. It's foolish to think that you are untouched by any of this. In this time of your engagement it may seem ridiculous that you could *ever* betray your partner's trust by being unfaithful, especially with one who is a close friend. But what makes you think you are exempt from the infidelities that destroy love and marriage all across the world? As far-fetched as the idea seems now, take the subject seriously. Take a little time for some role playing, now, as you think of these two scenarios that put trust to the test.

At a high school reunion you notice that a handsome fellow (the one voted most likely to succeed) has just joined the party, and through a crowd of admiring handshakes and high fives he has found his way straight to your wife. They were friends who dated in high school. After greeting you appropriately, he turns to your wife for nonstop catch-up conversation on the great old days and how much has happened since. As you patiently listen to the two matching memory for memory you realize that almost everything mentioned is news to you, especially all that chatter about what terrific times they had on dates. . . .

The second scenario is an afternoon hour at a resort where several couples — your good friends — have gathered for the weekend. When you come up from coffee with the girls, you notice your husband is not back yet from golf with the guys. You step out onto the room balcony for a moment of late afternoon sun on the water. To your surprise, there is your husband, strolling in leisurely conversation with one of the wives who missed the coffee. He's back in a half hour or so and meets you for dinner with the rest.

Now it's end of the evening time. You're both alone and there is a lull in the conversation. Do a bit of role playing. Has either of you felt a twinge of envy? Or left out? Or oversensitive? Is it important to you to get your thoughts and feelings out in the open? Easy or hard to do so? *Take some time now to imagine what you would say to each other.*

How strong is your trust level, as suggested by the role playing you've just done? Trust, of course, does not consist of words alone, but consistent deeds that reveal values that are the bedrock of trust. There is no substitute for *being* trustworthy, whether together or separated by the daily rounds of your lives. Being trustworthy, remember, is not an instant accomplishment but a constantly growing process of helping each other understand your strengths and vulnerabilities of character and attending to them with openness, courageous speaking, genuine listening, mutual forgiving, doing what builds trust and avoiding even the appearances of what erodes it. Thus you head off what otherwise chips away at you as a couple and the bond with friends, setting you adrift by real or

imagined annoyances, suspicions or downright mis-
trust without ever seeing what's happening or rem-
edying it. Over the years, you will be glad for the
trust building that frees you for friendships that
bless you a lifetime.

Respect is another prime element of friendship.

Respect for friends means granting them space
for their own thoughts, feelings, and preferences. It
means honoring them for what they do well and
telling them so. It means listening, which begins
with signaling to friends your readiness to hear
what they need to say. It is amazing how infrequently this is done and how many people are
rarely if ever asked what they're doing, thinking,
caring about, or needing to talk about. That's an
essential of friendship. It takes time, effort, tact,
and above all, genuine interest in the other, and
here is where couples help each other provide those
essentials.

Respect also means the courage to ask hard questions. "A friend is one who warns you" says a Jewish
proverb, and often it is friends who have earned the
respect required to get at things easy to leave alone
— where they can undermine and destroy. Such
hard questions are not accusations but inquiries
that show genuine care for the other. Often enough
it is friendship that can bear that burden, even
when family ties cannot.

Since we choose friends but have family, respect

for friends means the freedom also to go to them with the best and the least in your marriage. Friends who are truly friends accept your outreach not as an imposition but a recognition that they can help where others cannot. Respect for your friends enriches your love for each other as you share the deeper gifts and qualities that enrich not only your marriage but others as well, both married and single. In sharing them, joys are doubled and sorrows are half as heavy. In such sharing, God's grace is tasted, the grace that gives you friends who are sometimes closer than your closest relatives.

I want to pass along to you one small but practical idea for the maintenance of good friendships in marriage. It is the four minute rule. Years ago I learned this when caught up in a dreary and long church controversy (there are none worse) that could have eaten me up and made me a consummate bore to everybody. With my wife and closest friends I accepted the four minute rule, which limited talk about "the problem" to just four minutes a day. I recall being with best friends, talking like fury about the frustration and outrage of the situation, and then — as the four minute limit was reached — cutting off the subject for that day. Life did go on. We had other more important subjects to talk about. It was a sign of respect to keep the four minute rule, which can no doubt be longer or shorter. I speak from experience in saying that it not only

helps keep your sanity, it helps keep your friendships from an untimely death by boredom.

Communication

Basic in all that has been said so far, as well as to
what is coming, is communication. It is of huge importance and must not be taken for granted. It deserves much more attention than can be given it
here, and wiser heads than mine are worth consult-
ing. Nonetheless, see if the following helps you confirm what is good between you and helps you work
positively on what needs improving. What I say
here is so simple it risks being simplistic, yet at this
point brevity and clarity serve you well.

Think of communication at four levels in your
marriage.

The first is surface conversation, lightweight
talk that puts you at ease with each other. "Hi, how
are things?" "A good day at work?" "Shall we eat
out or eat in?" are examples of ways surface conversation gets going. It doesn't have to be profound,
witty, or entertaining. It's free and easy sharing of
what comes to mind but it's really more than super-
ficial. It's having your beloved to talk with and listen to about the routines of the day without wondering how every word and gesture is going over.
It's coasting along in casual, pleasant banter that

demonstrates how good it is to be in each other's company.

The second, deeper level is opened up in some way or another that means this: "I need you to listen." It's often introduced by a comment that tests the waters: "You'd never guess what happened today!" or "There's something on my mind of late." or "Is this a good moment for you to listen?" These are exploratory probes that announce a need and appeal for a hearing. If spoken in anger, however ("Look, here's the way it is and that's that!"), the effect is to stop communication immediately as the defenses go up. The other side of the problem is fear of venturing into this level where your vulnerability is bound to show. Be on guard against both barriers to communication when you need the other's undivided attention. Timing counts. Choose carefully when and where you seek this level with mutual benefit. It's a mark of love that you need your fiancée to hear you out at this level, which is no ploy or manipulation. It takes time to open yourself, especially when whatever bothers you is troublesome and not exactly flattering to yourself. Or maybe it's a puzzling concern that needs perspective, a decision you need to make together that can be great or small, or a dilemma with a long history that is finally getting an audience. Don't be fearful or discouraged that this comparatively early stage of communication between you makes you feel awkward. Remember that you have a lifetime of good communicating to work toward. Right now it's sufficient to lay a foundation appropriate to where you are.

Level three is the opposite of the above but involves the same dynamics. "Something on your mind？" "You don't seem to be yourself . . ." "If you're ready to talk I'm ready to listen . . ." are samples of communication openers that invite your loved one into this deeper level of mutual openness. It is one of love's surest signs. You really *want* to listen, to understand, to be there for the other, which is worlds away from intruding or insinuating or — worst of all — accusing. It comes from experience in reading the signals the other sends, sometimes unawares, by being preoccupied, reflective, moody, or uncharacteristically quiet. If your partner has had little experience in being invited to communicate at this level, or regards it as threatening, or has been long denied any such opening in previous relationships with people, the rule to follow is patience. Inviting is not badgering or meddling. It's simply the offer to listen, motivated by wanting to listen as the first step toward understanding and consensus in ensuing action on what is to be done. If you are the one invited, take it for what it is and cherish it as a golden asset in marriage. It ought not be spurned, for the climate love creates does not keep the other guessing about deeper matters that belong on, not under, the surface. A great deal is at stake here, nothing less than the quality of your present and future communication, something that opens you up as never before, encouraging, healing, and enabling your love to grow.

Level four is giving and taking, speaking and listening, offering the self and likewise receiving the other at the deepest level. Couples don't live at this level constantly. It is too intense. There's no magic formula in reaching this level. It combines all that the other three offer. It is known when each of you hears "This is how I see it — what do you think?" "Let me get this off my chest — and then listen to how it sounds to you." Perhaps you don't need words to tell of your arrival at this deep level. You know without words. It's not limited to monumental matters, either. It's good practice to experience this mutual give and take in matters as mundane as what to do next weekend, whose family to visit next holiday, or things more immediate such as negotiating the wedding invitation list, where to go for the honeymoon, and what a both-of-you-working schedule means when you are married and children come along.

Take time out now and talk over your communication at these four levels. It's best to cite examples of each. Where are you strongest? Where least communicative? Can you see now where you are in your communicating and where you want to be later on?

Conflict and arguments, in spite of the ugliness and damage they can cause, can nonetheless be turned into an occasion for much deepened communication. Your marriage vows are no insurance policy that your future is ever free of them. You already know something about missed communication and the upset it brings. Misgivings you may have now about arguing with each other in the future may stem from memories of dreadful family fights that have left scars. Or fears about conflict may arise from a sense of inadequacy to hold your own in tough moments or from a personality trait that would avoid conflict by any means rather than face it.

Think of a recent argument between you, or if the word argument doesn't fit, then some occasion when you were not happy with each other. Make sure it is specific enough for both of you to recall. Now revisit that moment with these questions:

Is it over? If not, what's holding you back from resolving it? Can you agree on what caused it? Are you both aware of what you are thinking and feeling about it now at this moment?

How did you experience the other's thought process and feelings when the heat was on? How did you experience your own? Sharp words? Impatient tone? Silent treatment? Tears? Body language?

If the matter is resolved, think of what went

into its resolution. Some couples deal with conflict then and there; others choose to let enough time pass to settle the dust before learning what really was going on. Strange though it sounds, it's essential to fight fair. Say (shout? murmur?) what you've got to get out in the open. Give your partner the same opportunity, which is plenty hard when emotions run high. Fighting fair means no penalties for being open, no grudges held that turn into time bombs later. How did you put the argument behind you? Can each of you say, genuinely, "I'm sorry, forgive me for hurting you, I didn't mean to"? If you haven't said it, can you say it now? It is an all-too-popular illusion that "love means never having to say you're sorry." To the contrary, love makes it possible to genuinely apologize and learn a lot in heading off similar collisions in the future.

The seriousness and straightforwardness with which you handle your conflicts has much to say about your readiness for marriage. It's no good to let them take you by surprise. It's all to the good to be honest now about yourselves and your will to settle them. A wise word from the New Testament puts it this way: "Be angry, but do not sin. Do not let the sun go down on your anger" (Ephesians 4:26). There is no pretending that there is no anger. Settling it before sundown, if not this one then one very soon, is all about not allowing anger to be nursed along toward peevishness or malicious wrath. Righteous anger is a healthy, galvanizing emotion of life. It is the other kind of anger that must be dealt with and overcome, lest it breed a mean-spirited, destructive surliness that keeps scores of past arguments and looks for the moment to get back. That is the death of love. Every marriage, especially yours, is worthy of the strengthening that comes from getting conflict out into the open, fighting fair, settling issues, forgiving mutually, and moving on — closer together than ever. Communication: everybody agrees it is important. But not all have a way to make it important. As you move on from this vital subject, be aware of where you both are strong and where the weak spots are. Your love is the motive for mutual growth in communicating.

Shared Interests

This happy subject is a very positive part of the larger picture of your compatibility. Each of you brings interests, preferences, and talents to your mutual enjoyment of each other's companionship. What are the pastimes, hobbies, and leisure time activities you already have learned to enjoy together? It's not a bad idea to make a list of them so far and to think together about those you've dreamed of doing someday but haven't had time or opportunity for yet.

I recall how early on in our marriage we began short camping outings, often with other couples. When our children arrived we took them with us to travel the country, showing them things we also enjoyed and doing so on a budget that worked. Not everyone is into the outdoors routine. Likewise with action sports, tastes in music and art, film preferences, television viewing habits, reading, walks, shopping (which to this day makes me yawn, I confess), and so the list grows as you add to it. Of course you have interests that are not shared. That's inevitable, and when pursued with mutual agreement and without excessive drain on time and money, such particular preferences make you more interesting persons and help you be at your best for each other. Allow for that and be glad for the other's skill at things you're not good at. But let me repeat the appeal to watch time carefully. This is even more applicable to work, which can take huge slices of time that should be devoted to each other. Help each other see what's getting out of hand and claiming far too much of your energies as well as time. Make time for each other and do so gladly, filling it with all that affords you fun, mutual appreciation, service to others, discovery of new ventures mutually enjoyed, and satisfying memories in later years.

Your unity of mind, then, is a channel of your love to flow freely as you handle money, relate to

family and friends, communicate, negotiate conflicts, and enjoy common interests. Compatibility
is too great a thing to be an instant creation. It is a
long-term and wonderfully creative quality that
you build together, confident that what you give
and take from each other now will mature as the
years pass, creating those rhythms of belonging together that give meaning to the ancient promise of
God: *"the two shall become one flesh"* (Genesis 2:24).

The Unity of Your Bodies

*Giving Yourselves to Each Other
as Male and Female*

You have bodies, male and female.

Thus you are sexual beings, a state of affairs that the Creator pronounced not only good but *"very good"* (Genesis 1:31). It is regrettable that the church has not always done well in spelling out this affirmation. If you are among those who have come to regard the Bible as a book of *Don't Even Think About It* or *You'd Better Not Or Else* in matters of sexuality, this chapter may appear as something to be done with as soon as possible. But stay open for surprises. You've been misled. On the other hand, you may be far more influenced by the bumper sticker morality of *If It Feels Good Do It* and the variations on that theme served up by our contemporary culture. That is an even greater fraud, parading under the façade of sexual freedom that is in fact sadly unfree.

Underlying this chapter is the belief that God has made your bodies in his image, which means for relationship to him and to each other. Sin has turned sexuality from a creation of beauty to a cause of anxiety. That's what happens when God-given love is exchanged for self-serving love, the better word for which is lust. But we humans are not abandoned to the ultimate emptiness of lust; bumper stickers notwithstanding. The cross of Jesus Christ is the good news of self-giving love as the power for sexual expression that blesses and builds you for a mutual, exclusive, and lasting commitment to each other. Fidelity is the beautiful result of that commitment and the key to sexual love that grows and deepens lifelong. Be humble in possessing such a treasure, if indeed you do. It is not everyone's experience. Those who hold to it and keep on working faithfully at it have no regrets. If what I have said so far sounds new or foreign to what you bring to this subject, I simply ask for an open mind. That's asking for a lot, not a little. Knowing the stubbornness and closed-mindedness of strong societal forces that flatten sex into advertising hype or cheapen it down to "casual sex" — a real put-down — it is well to know we're not in neutral territory here. Let's find our way between embarrassed taboo and anything goes.

The path we're seeking, sexual belonging through mutual self-giving, is hardly the majority view. Since the Fall, we humans bend sex, like everything else, inward upon ourselves. That's really what the serious word *sin* is about in spite of much confusion about its meaning. Thus sin ruins sexuality by either glamorizing it as the main force at work in humans or scorning it as essentially disgusting ("the cost is exorbitant, the pleasure fleeting, and the posture ridiculous," to quote G. K. Chesterton on sex for money). Self-centered sex, the endless quest for something or someone new to turn one on, leads finally to boredom with the whole business. Or nowadays to deadly disease. That's the last thing that should ever happen to a gift so basic and inherently good in God's sight. Along with boredom comes loneliness — ironically, the very loneliness that prompted this wrong-headed quest for self-serving pleasure in the first place. We catch hints of it in jokes about dirty old lecherous men, or women who have long since grown cynical after years of sleeping around. That's the fate of self-serving sex. I have seen its devastation. Perhaps you have, too. It's tragic. Never fun or funny. Never satisfying.

Something else needs saying up front in this conversation together. This book is not centered on sexual technique. That has its place. But there are better guidebooks for that important subject and I recommend that both of you browse through any good bookstore for the benefit of clear, well-written materials on this subject.

Nor does this conversation assume that you have had no sexual experience, carefully defined. No human being is without sexual experience in the sense of feelings, fantasies, needs, and experimenting with various forms of self-pleasuring. When it comes to sexual intercourse as the definition of sexual experience, that is a too narrow connotation of the frequently used phrase, "sexually active." Of course all human beings are sexually active, broadly understood. We're alive, aren't we! Sexuality is much more than technique and intercourse. That wider meaning is our present concern.

Here the center is on attitudes, motives, and the larger context of love, which grounds and blesses your sexual unity. That bond of trust, security, and loyalty comes from self-giving, not selfishness. Such is the setting that marriage provides. If you have chosen to express your love in sexual intercourse before marriage, and thus might be feeling defensive about what is said here, don't drop out or count the continuing conversation pointless. The conviction stated that full sexual sharing belongs in marriage need not stop everything or divert from what follows.

It's a good place to pause and check in with each other on what the above says or does not say to you. The point is getting at anxieties about sex, distinguishing between love and lust, and explaining the basis for fidelity. Is that worth talking about further?

Formative Experiences Early in Life

Your earliest childhood experiences in being "at home" with your body are important to recall and share. Did you grow up in a family where hugs, embraces, kisses were freely exchanged? Or was yours more reserved? Can you remember your family expressing affection to you and to each other in your presence? An important item I have learned over time is whether you received tactile affection from your father as well as mother. It is not that one is more important than the other. It is that more often than not, fathers have been less expressive to their children than mothers, with the misleading result that touch and embrace are seen as more womanly than manly. What you grew up with has much to do with how you view your body today. Since you are two persons who are going into your future very close to each other's bodies, you will do well to revisit early memories and tell stories that both amuse and inform you on this subject.

Let me tell a story that you must have some form or variation on yourself. I was about four or five. Beneath our back porch was a storage area for lawn tools, an ideal little clubhouse for the small fry up and down our block. One warm summer day a number of us gathered in our secret hideaway. Someone came up with the bright idea that we all take off our clothes. In no time flat our skinny bod-

ies were naked as jay birds. As I think back on it
now, it was both scary and fun. What I also recall is
my surprise that girls had no penis. My guess is that
the girls were equally surprised to find out that
their bodies were different from boys. Into that
mini-nudist camp walked my mother. Then, of
course, we were really scared. Instinctively, we were
suddenly more anxious than curious about our bare
bodies — an instinct to think about carefully. Without having to be told, we had a sense that something was wrong here, an echo down the long corri-
dor of time of the anxiety and for their unclothed
bodies that our primordial parents were said to experience after choosing self instead of God at the
center of life. Don't think of Adam and Eve as Vic-
torians. See in them the story of the body now become vulnerable to exploitation and abuse. Genesis
3 fills out the account. After my playmates dressed
in record time and lit out in all directions, my
mother did something of more lasting importance
for me than I could have realized at the time. She
took me up into our kitchen, sat me on her lap, and
gave me not a spanking but held me close as she patiently explained something of why we keep our
clothes on as a rule.

What came home to me in that early childhood
experience has to do with learning to be at home
with my body, beginning to sense the normal human curiosity about other people's bodies different

from my own, the strange attraction of that curiosity and the instinctive anxiety that accompanies discovery of that curiosity. I'm grateful to this day for a mother who started me out on a journey that could have pushed the instinct downward toward the old heresy that sex, as well as curiosity about it, is nothing but bad. Instead she chose actions that a four-year-old could understand positively, the reassuring warmth of holding me close to her bosom. I don't remember her words. Her affectionate embrace I do.

Another moment I recall — this time I was about eight — came when my father was helping me get an old coaster wagon back in running shape. Wanting to impress him with a slang term I had heard from older boys that I thought was cool and complimentary, I casually called the shined-up wagon a term that uses gutter language for oral sex. The look on his face told me instantly that I had chosen poorly, very poorly. But he did not punish me. Instead I can remember his patience with my embarrassed confusion. He sat me down and explained that some really ugly words can be used for things that deserve far better words, things I would understand later on. He didn't go into details for which I was not ready. It was another defining moment in my youth, the first time I became aware that matters of deepest sexual intimacy can be trivialized with lousy language.

Now is a moment for you to tell each other stories from your childhood. While we usually smile when hearing them, they are much more than amusing anecdotes or cute remembrances. They hark back to the beginnings of experiences that formed your emerging awareness of your body with its puzzling, fascinating capacities, and thus upon yourself as a sexual being. Healthy sexual unity in marriage grows out of being at home with your body, welcoming the mystery built into its graceful, humorous, and incredible capacities. It spares you the blight of letting your sexual unity sink down to humdrum routine or misusing it as a weapon against the other. *What stories of awakening sexuality come back to you, positively or negatively? How "at home" with your body were you as a child? And now as an adult?*

The Teen Years

Another benchmark to share along the way of your development is your coming into puberty and boy-girl relationships in your teen years.

For most of us that was a bittersweet time, a mix of awkwardness and fun, self-consciousness and blasé carefreeness. Who helped you understand and handle menstruation? Or who helped you untangle the puzzle of your first nocturnal emission of this strange new liquid in your body called semen. Entering puberty brings with it normal exploration of new capacities for sexual expression as an important part of love, its awkwardness notwithstanding. You are fortunate if a parent of some other trusted adult helped you begin to see it that way. Masturbation and other forms of self-pleasuring are all part of the passage from childhood to teen years. How did that passage go for you?

If it was marred by sexual abuse, the trauma of that violation must be healed. If not, the damage done will carry far into the coming years and directly hamper your capacity for free, fulfilling intimacy. This is because it is such a shattering betrayal of trust. Do not let it go untended. You are too important for that, and the trust level between you and the one you are to marry must be strong enough for you to open up dark memories. Even though some offender has left that terrible imprint on you that you are both dirty and guilty, you are not. The offender is.

Anything here that needs saying? Treat such conversation with great care, and encourage each other to seek more help beyond yourselves if necessary.

The Case for Fidelity and Commitment

It is out of the highest regard for sexuality that fidelity to each other is advocated here, as well as waiting until marriage for sexual intercourse. I realize that many see it otherwise and you may be among them. In listening to many couples through the past four decades of huge change in sexual attitudes and practice, I am aware of how poorly we Christians have made the case for waiting until marriage for full sexual sharing of love. It is not clear by any means that such an intimate expression of love is a sign of Christ's own fidelity to us (Ephesians 5:25-33 is good reading on the subject). The point is that sexual intercourse is placed within the circle of the wide range of unity in marriage which includes bills paying, grocery shopping, worshiping God, entertaining friends, earning an income, caring for others in need, forgiving each other, working together at good causes beyond yourselves, enjoying shared interests, discovering new ones, and in all of these things trusting each other for the rest of your lives together. Christ's fidelity to us is the basis for your mutual fidelity, which grows in its dignity, beauty, and deep fulfillment as the years pass.

Another issue that needs straightforward attention is the choice to live together before marriage. Two reasons are most often given by couples who make this choice: economics and compatibility. It's cheaper to live together, no doubt about it. And it seems to make sense that two people ought to find out whether they are right for each other before getting married.

Both reasons and others that can be added miss the point: commitment. In the Christian view of marriage, commitment draws upon a source deeper than yourselves. It is based on God's prior commitment to us, in spite of all the ways we fall short. Commitment means access to the power that sees us through when we're at an impasse with each other or when the checkbook balance calls for waiting instead of having it all now. Commitment means love can still be recovered, even though a couple cannot be in love at the moment. Any couple married for any length of time knows that they not only survived tough times but came through them deeper, finer persons because their character met the test. That doesn't happen on a trial basis, for then we humans quit too soon. We lack the tools to work with. The truth is: marriage sustains love. Love does not create marriage. It draws from God, who creates and sustains marriage by the love that brought his son to the cross and raised him from death so that the sin that destroys is overcome.

Commitment is no cheap accomplishment, nor is it celebrated in the current popular culture, so eroded by casualness in the face of things deep and dear. With instant gratification coming at us from all sides, it is not surprising that waiting till marriage to live together seems pointless. What is missing, however, is the belief that marriage is a God-given covenant, a witness to his purpose of working for the greater good for both of you and through your marriage for the wider good of family, friendship, congregation, and community.

By waiting you are saying that something as momentous as living together in a lifetime of fidelity takes the grace of God as the power for your mutual hard work. If this conforms to your standards, stick with it and I cheer for you. If what I have said does not, the conversation need not end here. Christian care does not close the book on people who want a good marriage but have made other arrangements not supported by what I have been saying. I'll accept the fact that the church has too often alienated people by stating rules with no reasons underneath that have to do with love, truth, and humility for our own shortcomings. If you can accept the fact that decisions to live together are more a reflection of our self-centered culture than the divine Word flatly opposed by that culture, we can proceed.

What's important to think through and talk over at this point, regarding this subject? Can we go ahead, much more conscious of the essential meaning of commitment?

Let me invite your thinking at this moment to the marriage rite in which you will participate. In many marriage services, in some form or another, this truth is expressed: *God has made us male and female and established marriage as the cornerstone of all human community.* This is a truth of huge importance, worth your careful attention now as a step toward the deeper experience of marriage that you seek. Marriage is "the cornerstone of all human community," which points to your covenant together as not only deeply personal but meant for the wider good that makes for human community rather than human chaos. Can you use a few minutes now to talk with each other about what such vision means to you, how you've seen it working in marriages you admire, and what practical steps you now foresee as ways to implement that vision?

Levels of Intimacy

This time of courtship is a wonderful time for shared affection. Your devotion and tenderness with each other now is building your love to keep on growing long into the future, a future that can sometimes seem daunting. It's natural to ask how attractive you will be to each other ten or fifty years from now. The positive answers begin now, as you accept where you are and as you grow in the sheer delight of being ever closer to each other.

Pay attention to each other's signals. You develop ways of letting each other know that you'd really welcome a kiss or embrace or just being close without having to talk at all. If sending and receiving such signals is less than perfect now, be patient.

What counts is not only the awareness of romantic desire and expression, but the general climate of respect, thoughtfulness, good humor, and sincerity in genuine care for each other's needs. In that setting your affection, tenderness, and passion will grow. Without it, it won't grow. Indeed, it won't survive.

Despite the have-it-all-now mind-set, there is much to be said for shyness and timing in romantic exchange through courtship and engagement. It's an almost forgotten art. But growing slowly in levels of intimacy gives you time to connect your sexuality to other values that enhance and deepen your appreciation of the physical side of your love for each other. Shyness is, after all, tantalizing. It is mutually stimulating to you both first to dream, envision, and fantasize before the reality of your sexual bond is known in the fullness of marriage. As Winston Churchill once said in another context, anything worth doing is worth starting clumsily. So what if you are not Don (or Donna) Juan¿ Give yourselves time. Sexuality and its expression are more subtle, spontaneous, and teasing than most of the how-to manuals would imply. The key to excitement is in what is hidden, more than in what is revealed. Above all, sexuality thrives on trust of the other, a trust based on demonstrated goodness and consistency of faithful devotion to each other. That takes time and is worth all the time it takes. You don't get that from most movies, novels, or television portrayals of love — which depend on bed hopping to get your attention.

There are better guides to shape your dreams and desires. Choose according to your values and pace your growth toward full sexual expression as your time of marriage arrives. Don't buy into the notion that all this is sexually repressive. It comes, in fact, from the healthiest regard for sex as a great gift of the Creator.

As a practical way to prepare for your full sexual intimacy, read (if possible, together) clear and positively written guidebooks on sexual love. Too many men do not fully understand the erogenous zones of their loved one's body, and the same may be true for women. For the sake of your happiness, both of you need to know that sexual arousal begins in the brain, not the genitals. It has to do with the importance of imagination and fantasy, in the marvelous mystery of why and when arousal comes. All tender touch is then sensuous and welcome. The erogenous zones of your body as a woman — lips, mouth, breasts, vagina, clitoris, and the skin overall — are for caressing, touching, and tender stroking in preparation for intercourse.

As a rule, woman's arousal is more subtle and sustained than a man's. Over the years, in listening to many wives with marital problems, I have often heard this: "My husband needs to understand the importance of tenderness as well as passion. I can be sexually content sometimes even if I don't always experience orgasm in our lovemaking . . ." "If only he would just hold me, be gentle with me, caress me, and speak his love to me I would be glad." That must be heard. You need to be free to tell your husband that. That's the only way he can know of your deep pleasure.

Your body as a man, like the female body, begins its sexual desire in the brain. The path of transmission of desire is a wondrous work of the Creator who has endowed your body with intricate networks to suffuse your whole being with powerful feelings. There is less subtlety in your male signals of sexual excitement. The rush of blood into your genitals creates that amazing, mysterious, but hardly subtle result: the erect penis.

It is sad to hear a husband speak, often with an anxious sense of personal failure, of his wife's reluctance or refusal to touch and caress his body, in particular his erogenous areas. Given the basic ways of being clean through bathing and free of genital disease, there is no good reason for a wife to withhold touch and word that both arouse and reassure her husband. Such gentle and prolonged foreplay is appropriate to full sexual union between husband and wife. It is faithful use of the capacity God has given both husband and wife for their mutual pleasure and deep satisfaction in marriage.

As to time and place of sexual expression, let me

invite you to imagine this scenario a year or more from now. It's a Saturday morning. For several hours you and your spouse have been painting walls in your bedroom. Wife is on the ladder, painting the ceiling. Husband is down below, mixing the next batch. It's warm. Wife slips off her blouse. Husband sees the beauty of wife's body. He's warming up, too. Husband suggests a break; the bed is there waiting. Wife comes down from ladder, happily excited. The walls get painted later.

I have not invented this scene, but remember it from a conversation with a couple who shared it with love and good humor. What stays with me about it is their recognition of how hesitant and tentative the signal sending can be. He didn't want to come across as a sexual glutton, nor did she. But one didn't brush off the other in a moment when arousal was real. That's the great thing in the physical side of love. It invites spontaneity, openness, passion, humor, lightheartedness, and compatibility.

I think of another couple and their story. To look at them one would guess they have it all: handsome, well off, and happy together. The appearances are deceiving. They are anything but happy. It began on the last day of their honeymoon with a missed signal. She commented on the hour they had before checkout time, and somewhat shyly suggested that the romantic setting might have a very good use for their closing hour in a beautiful place. He missed her need altogether, and dismissed it with an offhand comment that made her feel foolish for honestly letting her desire be known. The embarrassment festered into resentment, producing anger, resulting in retaliation. It has been six months since this couple has had sexual relations and they are fighting for their marital lives. Indeed, the problems are deeper than sexual. But it began casually, around a seemingly teasing request that was thoughtlessly shunned.

This wounded couple emphasize the importance of reading the signals. Take care with each other. Attend to the other's sexual needs in marriage. If the time and mood are mutually right, help the other catch on without embarrassment or rejection. If the time is not right, make it clear that a better time is coming — soon. Love will bear that. What love cannot bear is the idea that sexual arousal itself is wrong, dirty, or mere duty. How could it be? Who created this fantastic capacity in both of you?

Accept your bodies for what they are, nothing less than God's premier handiwork. Sin defaces that handiwork to be sure. But Christians live by forgiveness and in grace. That means the freedom to possess each other with passion, tenderness, humor, fidelity, in the power of that love which flows into life through Christ Jesus. He means good for you, and is happy in your happiness. In this deeply personal aspect of your coming marriage, look forward to growth and maturing as the years come and go. Be humble in the awareness that both of you are vulnerable to temptations that seem unthinkable now.

In a hopeful vision of your future, but also one that is hard for you to catch now, I ask you to envision yourselves when you are in your eighties or more, still with a light in your eye for each other. It is a crowning achievement to reach that stage, alive and with a lively love for each other that has not tarnished but mellowed through the years. Not long ago a couple celebrated their golden wedding anniversary, beginning the grand event with a service of thanksgiving in church. There they sat in the front row, with several generations of family around them and friends old and new. They were holding hands. That said much. It was a visible sign of that unseen bond of enduring love that made them glad and all of us glad with them. In spite of the inevitable limits of the body — our sexuality is earthbound — the vows they spoke a half century ago are alive and well. *Can you see yourselves building now toward such a crowning moment fifty years from now?*

Becoming Parents

Sexual unity is, of course, the way we forge new links in the chain of the generations. Your cohabitation in marriage is the way children are born and your love forms the space in which they grow with security and confidence into their future. Thus your sexual unity is given a purpose and dignity which is your high calling as parents. In your romance now, you have the bliss of each other. In bringing children into the world you are placed at your post of responsibility that is second to none. In no other way than through good marriage can children be brought to fitness for good living in the world they will help shape.

The decision, then, to seek to become parents is momentous. You can't take it for granted that you will have children, for here again we do not write the script. Childlessness is a possibility and is a heavy burden for those who long for children of their own. It is better by far to approach the prospect of having children with humility, prayer, maturity, and good planning. Yes, diapers and night feeding, crying at any hour, are among the intrusions that a baby makes upon you without asking your permission. But these realities cannot replace the great miracle that parenthood is, and the lasting joy of seeing your children grow into lives that honor God, bless others, and bring deep peace to your own hearts.

In this era of two-job, two-career families it is too shortsighted to assume that all those hours of consigning your child to the care of others takes no toll. Children suffer from the loss of the irreplaceable love and nurture that only both of you can supply. One or the other must be on hand full time at home for your child who depends on you for everything.

When death or divorce or loss of health or injury make it impossible for the remaining parent to carry the full load, then this appeal cannot apply. The single parent who works hard to raise a family deserves nothing but respect and support. But when it is choice rather than circumstance that makes young parents put career over child rearing, everybody loses. Above all, the child is deprived of the hands-on care that is basic for the rest of life. And from what I see, parents suffer as well. Caring for a baby and keeping a full-time job outside the home is exhausting. With that exhaustion much of the quality goes out of marriage. It may be the husband who is Mr. Mom at home rearing the child. But please make it one or the other.

Look with extra care at the factors that make it easy to dismiss this appeal. Is it maintaining a lifestyle or fulfilling what long years of education have prepared you for? Your child is not raised well by a lifestyle or an educational success story. Full-time parents are what your child needs, parents who give priority of time, effort, love, and guidance by example. It's a good time to talk it through.

Where are we on the subject of children? What priority will we put on raising them? Which of us does what? How will children affect our job/career plans?

One of the most tragic casualties of the two-career marriage is the situation in which one spouse — most often but not always the wife — works hard outside the home and does whatever share of parenting leftover time and energy allow, only to be abandoned later by a spouse who left the marriage for someone else. Look that outrage squarely in the eye now and be ever so clear that neither you nor your children are going to set yourselves up for that heartbreak. Two-career marriages are a highly endangering species that contribute more to the divorce rate than to lasting fulfillment. It is always the children who suffer the most. It takes minimally ten years for a child to get over the ending of a marriage. Children do not will themselves into existence. We do that as adults.

The statement is so obvious it sounds trite. Nonetheless it is true: becoming parents marks a sea change in your marriage. In planning for parenthood, let nothing undermine the priority you establish in carrying out life's foremost calling: parenting your offspring with the best you are and the best you have.

In an age of widespread pre-marital sex it may

sound odd to advocate a good medical consultation on matters of contraception. But there are couples who wait until marriage before cohabiting, and if you are among them do not think of yourselves as fossils. Preparation for this aspect of marriage calls for your good judgment. Do you both agree that using contraceptives is in order? If one has reservations, the other needs to respect that. I see no moral reason for not practicing birth control. You do yourselves and your children a favor by being well prepared for the responsibilities of parenthood.

Which of you will use a contraceptive? Do both of you agree to the wisdom of a complete physical before marriage and to making the necessary medical appointments?

If one or both of you has experienced sexual intimacy before marriage there is something that needs saying. Perhaps that way of life was assumed because no one ever thought enough of you to sit down and make the moral case for waiting. You are not responsible for what was not given you, though you do bear a responsibility to your conscience. There is in all of us a deep-rooted sense that somehow this act of deepest intimacy has a good deal more to it than the act itself. Thus there may be an unspoken sense that intercourse before marriage carries a penalty with it that will somehow, someday, doom your marriage. While this voice of conscience may be so anesthetized that the very thought of it makes no sense at all, something more elemental than current fads and cultural acceptance can still speak to you. Whatever form this has taken before, it now needs to be heeded and not dismissed as a relic of a time long gone.

You need only take seriously the thought that if sexual intimacy was acceptable before marriage with someone else, why couldn't you or your fiancée make room for a similar intimacy with another person now or in the future? The answer usually heard is that this won't happen because of love for each other. But wasn't that the reason before?

Why bring all this up? It is to avoid rationalizing previous arrangements instead of meeting the present situation with the only real answer to the problem: the grace of Christ our Lord. He forgives, not rationalizes, our sins. His mercy is never forced on us, but never refused us when we ask for it from the heart. We who know our need for his undeserved favor find here the freedom from anxious self-justifying and self-deception. It is essential for your future — whatever your past has been — to be secure and free in the greatness of the divine love that made all things from the beginning and holds it all together now and always. Your bodies are the temple of the Holy Spirit. Look forward to welcoming each other, as Christ has first welcomed you, to his glory and your lasting good.

Souls United in Marriage

In turning the conversation now to the unity of your souls in marriage, I am aware that we don't talk much about the soul anymore. It is easier to craft a conversation on the stock market, the latest fashions, or sports scores than it is to open up our souls to each other in ways both natural and meaningful.

But let's come to this center of the whole subject of marriage without hesitation or wondering if there might be some way to skip it. It comes last, not because it is least, but because it is foundational to everything said beforehand.

Building a Spiritual Foundation

Your love for each other needs such a foundation. It must stand and withstand much at present and so much more in the future. In the previous conversations we've referred to the essential importance of common values. Now let's take time to focus on the spiritual unity that gives life, freshness, and durability to your love and loyalty.

Each of you has a soul. What does that mean? It means that God has created you with the capacity to respond to him and to each other spiritually. In spite of the catastrophic intrusion of sin which distorts and defaces God's image in you, you are nonetheless his children in Christ, whose cross and resurrection are God's good news in every bad situation that sin creates. You are not orphans, wondering if there is any lasting meaning in life or power to enter into it. You are loved and accepted. The coming of the Holy Spirit through the word of Christ's grace, the sacraments he has given his church, and the surprises of his grace experienced in relationships with people is what empowers you for spiritual life in general and now, particularly, for the spiritual unity of marriage.

This aspect of marriage is easiest to overlook.

The reasons vary. Here are several worth thinking about for their application to the present conversation.

It may be that you do not think of yourself as a religious person, or that your view of being a religious person is negative. People often drift into this view of themselves after spiritually lean times in adolescence and early adulthood. Strange, isn't it, how we can become exiled from the certainties of childhood — how the things we treasure most when very young are exactly the things we scorn as teenagers and young adults. Little kids are often conscious of God in ways that adults miss: they sing to God, talk to God, see God all around them. Yet these budding believers are often ready to graduate from church by the time they're in eighth grade.

Reaction to loveless religion in childhood or teen years can be the result of heavy-handed church life or pastoral mishandling. That reaction becomes a time bomb in young adults who have chucked it all as kid stuff. Or it may be that one has had no spiritual guidance as a child against which to react. Some crisis may have stirred a rebellion against God, who may have seemed distant or silent at the time. Most often it happens that spiritual life is stunted not because God is denied but because he is moved off to the margin of busy lives, or turned into a number called only in emergency. God is not spoken of, at least with any naturalness. To be sure, it is not always this way. Generalizations about young adults are unfair. There are too many vibrant young men and women of faith who are anything but marginal in faith and practice.

What about us in regard to experience with God and talk of matters of faith? This is a good time to speak of past spiritual life in family and congregation — or the lack of it and why. Remember, it's not to make points or pass judgment, but to understand each other as persons with souls.

Whatever your spiritual past has been or not been, here is the point of spiritual unity. It is the foundation for all else and gives your marriage a quality that comes in no other way. And isn't this what you want, a marriage with a solid foundation for the best quality possible? A marriage that comes from being at your best for each other spiritually, and making your unity of soul the motivating power for a life together that is anything but humdrum and hand over hand? Unity of soul is not dependent on belonging to the same denomination or having identical religious upbringing, important though these are. It comes from your standing before God, your response to his truth and love, and your desire to share him with each other.

Man and woman you are, each of you unique, called in marriage to bring that uniqueness into a bond the Bible calls "one flesh." The idea is a total unity of your lives, a living and growing unity that is meant for companionship and for service to others. Don't depend on financial affluence to accomplish this. Nor will sexual prowess bring it off. Spiritual life together is the channel through which this center is established. Such unity is God's handiwork in you, enabling each of you to respond first to his incredible goodness and then to each other in ways that build your faith and increase its fruits of love, joy, peace, patience, kindness, goodness, gentleness, faithfulness, and self-control. What marriage doesn't need these fruits?

A foundation for marriage in spiritual unity, then, is hardly a sideline item that may be interesting to people who are the religious kind. Rather, it is the very essence of marriage itself. See it, both of you, as your best and most practical possession. It means not only your mutual happiness, but your life together as a glory to God and for the larger good of those whose lives you touch.

Marriage as a Mutual Ministry

See your marriage in its depth and dignity as God establishes you as partners in a vocation. That important word comes from the Latin *vocare,* meaning "calling." Another useful word to describe the spiritual framework for your life together is ministry, with its root meaning as serving. The words vocation and ministry are not limited to ordained people but bear a direct reference to your lives united in the calling to serve God and the sphere of life you touch and influence in a multitude of ways. The basic idea is that your marriage has a far greater purpose to it than your own personal happiness.

Perhaps the point becomes clearer by imagining

someone asking you "Why do you want to marry each other?" "Because we love each other and want to be happy" is an obvious answer. That's fine, but it doesn't go far, wide, and deep enough. As persons who believe that God seeks to make marriage the cornerstone of all human community — the phrase from many marriage services mentioned earlier — your marriage is a building block for the wider good of others beyond yourselves. This by no means discounts your love for each other and your personal happiness. It supports it. In fact, it may not be overstating the matter to say that it ensures your happiness, as it turns you outward in service rather than confining it only to yourselves.

How does this happen? It occurs through your mutual support for each other's serving in ways suited to your talent and time. That includes things like volunteering in a hospital or home for the aged, coaching a kids' sports team, being a den mother, serving on a local school board, teaching Sunday school, delivering Meals on Wheels, tutoring youngsters needing help with schoolwork, singing in a parish choir, chaperoning youth outings, and the list goes on. Each of these things takes time and energy. When done by one of you, the agreeable support of the other is essential. It won't do to commit to such wider service with pressure against it from your spouse. Wisdom and timing are essential in knowing when, where, and how a couple is ready for this commitment. When marriage is viewed as a calling for serving the wider good of community and congregation, then ministry to each other means encouragement, interest, and active coopera-tion in doing what is necessary to see to it that the marriage is not strained but strengthened by put-ting time and talent to work for the good of others.

Normally, a couple with this motivation grows into actions of wider service. It is unwise to make major commitments of time and effort during the early stages when you are establishing yourselves, growing together, and discovering the pace and style of your life together. We learn a lot about this wider purpose of marriage from others who practice it. An example in our earlier years of marriage was foster care of infants and young children. We had seen how much that meant through close friends who had opened their doors to children without home or family. Over time our own four children learned to change diapers and feed infants as young as a week old, as our family became a transition place for babies and young children preparing for adoption. It was a phase in our marriage that brought mutual blessing. Marriages have seasons, and wider service is often geared seasonally. Dads and moms coach, mentor, etc. as their own children are into Scouting or Little League. Couples taking on leadership in young married groups of a congre-gation are often at that time in their own lives.

Couples who reach retirement put their time and talent to good purpose because the golden years offer more than shuffleboard.

How about our vision of what our marriage is for? *Are the words* vocation *and* ministry *in relation to marriage new to you? Are they worth exploring for the promise they hold for your future? What do we already know from experience about serving each other and others as the key to fulfillment?*

Sometimes couples preparing for marriage express this sense of wider vocation in their wedding vows. It can find a voice in the homily spoken by the one officiating in the wedding service. It must not be overlooked to say that both of you standing together at the altar on your wedding day represent a hugely important vocation on the part of your parents seated in the front row. They, and others with them, are key building blocks in bringing you to this point in your lives. Now it is your turn to add new links to the chain of blessing others as well as yourselves. Whether or not the wedding service specifically expresses this vision, the main thing is that at least a glimmer of this magnificent, wider vision of marriage is in your minds and hearts as you look ahead. If that is there, you will surely find myriad ways to express it. You will find fulfillment in ways you can only dream of now. And others will flourish because the ministry of your marriage has reached them and made a lasting difference for good.

All this calls for faith as the basis for the values that you share with each other. Faith in the living God is indeed a living, active power that protects you against the drift into drabness and taking each other for granted. It is the dynamic center that keeps your love fresh for each other and fruitful for others. What values are we talking about? St. Paul offers these to take to heart: compassion, kindness, humility, meekness, patience, mutual forgiveness, peace, gratitude, creative goodness, faithful actions, and above all — the love that God puts into our hearts through Jesus Christ his son (Colossians 3:12-17). This does not exhaust the possibilities. But it's a good start. As a rule, we don't get much help from outside the community of faith in these matters. The forces of self-serving, over-indulging personal preferences, shallow vision, and values based on money and "toys" are stronger than we tend to recognize. Be aware of them. They do not help. They hinder and can finally destroy what you fondly hope for now.

What can we share with each other that helps toward understanding both strengths and weaknesses in previous religious experience?

Communicating Upward — Together

Let me suggest another aspect of the previously mentioned subject of communication: prayer.

Prayer is communication of the first order of importance. It is communicating upward to God, who puts us on speaking terms with himself through the inner working of his Spirit. Those who pray together in marriage have a treasure that more people need to discover. It is a subject more caught than taught. If you have been a guest in a home where simple, genuine thanks was offered to God for the food that sustains life and for all the good that comes from fellowship around a table, you might well recall the impact of that experience. Why not consider putting it into practice, if you have not already begun to do so?

You desire a suitable house or condo in which to live? Why not build a spiritual home with prayer together? You are already thinking about furnishings. Why not furnish the walls of your minds and hearts with a faith, hope, and love that nothing can destroy? You need to pay attention to the value of dollars you earn and invest. Why not value the gifts of the Spirit that infuse your marriage with a quality that others will see and want to emulate?

Mealtime prayers are most often the best way to start, remembering that time around the table is prime time for each other, never to be neglected or taken for granted. Simple prayers, thanking God for life and food and the love that holds you together, are best spoken simply and from the heart. Set prayers, on the other hand, give you what you want to say to God but are not quite sure how. Here are samples:

The eyes of all wait upon you, O Lord, and you give them their food in due season. You open your hand and satisfy the desires of every living thing. Amen.

Lord God, heavenly Father, bless us and these gifts which we receive from your bountiful goodness, through Jesus Christ our Lord. Amen.

I remember a prayer that our family prayed from my earliest childhood which we still pray and pass on to others:

We thank Thee, heavenly Father, for all our earthly good, for home and health and clothing, and for our daily food. Amen.

When children enlarge the family circle, you are their best teachers of prayer by practicing it. Thus little children learn from you to fold their hands, bow their heads in reverence (reverence: one more great thing in life not learned from television), fold their hands and say: *God is great, God is good, and we thank him for this food. Amen.*

Little children can be our teachers of prayer. Once small children learn to speak or sing a table prayer, they are free to call to attention the adults who in forgetfulness or adult busyness have begun passing the food around with no word of thanksgiving. "Hey, we didn't pray yet!" is a cry not to be ignored. I've seen a whole table of adults respond with belated, though sheepish head nodding. Thus it happens that for the umpteenth time in history, little children become our models of faith.

Is prayer before meals a practice you have known earlier? Continuing now? Can it have a regular place in your anticipation of the daily routines of your marriage?

Prayer together sanctifies coming moments of greatest happiness. To speak your deepest joy and thanksgiving with your spouse is to double it. Prayer is the anchor that holds you when crisis hits like a thunderbolt and everything seemingly nailed down breaks loose. What can you say in an emergency room at three in the morning when your life partner is threatened with death, eyes wide with fright, and begs you speak to God? Prepare now for the brightest and the darkest passages of life that are surely coming. Put into practice now this great gift of God we call prayer, the foundation for which our Lord Jesus gave us in the prayer that begins . . . "Our Father who art in heaven. . . ." Can you complete it? Allow yourselves the experience of hearing each other's voices united in speaking to God. Can this be the start of a deepened spiritual relationship that you can carry into the future? *Is this a good time for a quiet pause in your conversation to pray aloud together?*

Mutual prayer and all spiritual graces for your marriage are encouraged and deepened by regular worship in a congregation. Do you come from different denominations? Or from little or no church background at all? The subject is worth attending to now.

Finding Your Church Home

If you each have meaningful connections in different congregations presently, it is important for each of you to go to church in both places together in order to learn more of what that tradition means in your respective religious experience. Meet each other's pastor or priest. Talk with that person about your marriage and learn what that tradition can contribute to your mutual good. If one or the other has no present congregation connection, begin searching for a church home together. The criteria you should establish are soundness in the Christian gospel of the crucified and risen Lord, evidences of the fruits of love in the way people worship and work together, a sense of Christian mission to the community and beyond, clergy leadership that is welcoming, and signs that the congregation can be a place where you both can be spiritually well served and find your niche of serving others.

The congregation connection really does count.

We live in an era when many disagree, however. A prevailing view of religion regards it as private opinions rather than a community of faith with commitments. Spirituality is popular though rarely defined. Church and congregation in this view, however, are optional, and many opt out. Too often core beliefs of Christians through the ages are rejected without ever having been genuinely experienced. People can carry minimal or negative childhood experiences of Sunday school into adulthood, never outgrowing them through spiritual maturing. Not infrequently, congregations and clergy themselves have been part of the problem. It is also true that people have never given the church a chance.

Whatever the obstacles may be, as people who are preparing for marriage you can welcome this time in your lives as unusually promising for rededication and renewal of your relation to God. That is the motive for serious attention to finding a church home together where Christ gathers you anew into his body, the church. Such a congregation is where you can worship him in reverence and joy, where you both learn the deep grace of Sabbath-keeping that makes Sunday an oasis of refreshment for soul and body, preparing you well for whatever the following week might bring. You both can be a powerful and positive influence on each other in establishing the rhythms of Sabbath worship and weekday life, learning how each needs the other and both fit together. This is not automatic, nor is it always easy. It calls for the best you both can give it. God intends great good for you in your marriage. Open up to him. Let him work in you and through you, recognizing that marriage is prime time for new beginnings in the depth of your souls. Thus you are building now those foundations that will serve you a lifetime. With no illusions about the absolutely lethal forces that work against all this, put the goal of an active and growing faith at the very center of your priorities.

Never let religious differences, past or present, become occasions for argument or conflict. Nothing is won by "winning" spiritual arguments. Nor can faith and its commitments be forced. The example of your Christian faith and action speaks for itself. Let God do the persuading. Please don't keep him waiting.

Meaningful worship and service in the congregation is vital to making your household a place where God is at work in the daily rounds of your life together. The Word you hear and the sacraments you receive equip you to love each other in spite of the faults and failings that inevitably appear as the ups and downs of life come along. Tempers that can flare are calmed. Those magic words — "I'm sorry" — are spoken and heard. Disagreements do not develop into serious rifts. Forgiveness is received and given. Peace reigns over chaos. Mutual respect grows. Truth-speaking has a chance. Life grows vastly more interesting. Commitments are kept. Fidelity has solid footing. New paths of service are sought. Happiness is real. A deepening sense of the sheer goodness of being together keeps on growing. Isn't this what you want? This, for sure, is what the heavenly Father wants you to have.

Talk of how you see connections between Sunday worship and weekday life fit together. Tell each other of your experiences with congregation(s), both positive and negative. Are you open to spiritual growth? To finding a church home?

Till Death Parts You

A final word about something most assuredly final.

In your marriage vows you promise yourselves to each other "till death parts us."

I have known times when couples have asked to drop that somber phrase from the wedding service. Strangely, and without morbid intent, the phrase belongs and should not be removed. That is so because it is true, and the wedding service should be truthful also about this part of the larger meaning of marriage.

God means marriage for earth, not heaven. Why? Because in heaven we have God in the blessed fullness of the Holy Trinity — Father, Son, and Holy Spirit — the source of all life and love. On earth God intends marriage to be a sign of that coming fullness. Husbands and wives are called to love each other as Christ loves the church and gave himself for her (Ephesians 5:25). This magnificent truth is meant to come true in all the years that you have each other as husband and wife. They do come to an end. But here the meaning of "end" is not that everything stops. Rather it is that everything good and true and hopeful in your marriage is not stopped, but fulfilled in that life which our risen Lord has gone ahead to prepare.

Among the many great things our Lord is accomplishing in your marriage is this one: you are helping to prepare each other for eternity. Think about that phrase. It is not the most obvious answer, is it, to the question of why get married? But the deep wellsprings of God's truth at work in human hearts have many things that, though not obvious, are nonetheless meant to be claimed and applied.

As remote as it seems, try to envision the time coming when death will part you. What is it that the dying one can hold onto and find comfort in? Better stated, Who is it that is present in that fearful hour? It is the God who has been with you each step of the way, never forgetting you, never indifferent to your needs both great and small. When this witness comes at the last, the witness that has been steadfastly present through the years, the remaining spouse has something of incomparable worth to give the one for whom death approaches. In the face of panic, irrelevance, false hope, or numbed silence, a parting blessing is given at the last, consistent with the spiritual life that has been building all along.

Likewise, the one who must die has something to give the beloved partner who soon shall face a whole new way of life, alone. It is the peace of God that keeps the partner who lives on. That peace has been no stranger in the marriage. It has been known in many ways in the marriage, through worship, prayer, the Word, congregational participation, service of all kinds, witness, acts of reconciliation, deeds of sacrificial care — and countless more. Becoming a new widow or widower is entering into a new time of life for which there has been preparation. In that assurance, a spouse whose days are ending can die in the hope that God holds fast the beloved partner that mortal arms, weakened by disease or age, can no longer hold.

Be thankful for the youthful vitality of your lives now. But do not think it is permanent. An end comes. But through eyes of faith it can be seen as a bridge to a new beginning that God has promised. Faithful, fulfilling marriage is a sign of the eternal covenant by which Christ loves the church, and calls husband and wife to love each other accordingly. If all this is unclear or distant-sounding now, so be it. Later on you will know. And that knowing will be known because you have shown each other that marriage is built upon the divine love that is eternal. Living it is the way to learn it.

And now that this point in talking marriage together is reached, it may be best to think in quiet about the things read, thought about, and discussed.

My thanks to you for letting me join you as an interested outsider to your conversations. May I suggest that a good way to conclude is to speak this prayer together:

Blessed God, prepare us well for a life together that pleases you, blesses us, and serves others. Through Christ your Son, who sanctified the wedding at Cana by his presence, we ask your grace upon our marriage and these days of preparing. We thank you for the promise of your Holy Spirit to unite us by Christ's love in mind, body, and soul, now and in the years to come. Amen